UNSTOPPABLE

How Jim Thorpe and the
Carlisle Indian School Football Team
Defeated Army

written by **ART COULSON**
illustrated by **NICK HARDCASTLE**

CAPSTONE EDITIONS
a capstone imprint

The morning sun shone brightly. As it climbed in the sky, it warmed the grass in front of Keokuk Hall on the Haskell Institute campus. This day in mid-January 1900 was warmer than usual in Lawrence, Kansas. It would be a special day at the boarding school for American Indian students.

Today one of the best football teams in the country would visit Haskell. The Carlisle Indian Industrial School team had been riding on trains since Christmas, when it had beaten the best team in the West, the University of California. On a three-week trip back to Pennsylvania, the Carlisle team stopped at several American Indian boarding schools. Today was Haskell's turn.

All the Haskell boys gathered in their uniforms for a dress parade. The girls wore their best dresses and stood huddled together. The crowd buzzed with excitement.

The Haskell students came from many different tribes. They spoke dozens of different languages. But they were united in their love for the new sport of football.

One short, skinny 12-year-old with dark, wavy hair stood off by himself.
He tossed a battered homemade football in the air and caught it.

He squinted into the sun as he watched the Carlisle players stride across the
lawn to the dining hall. He dreamed of one day playing alongside them.

The boy, whose mother called him Wa-tho-huk—Bright Path—in his native
Sauk language, also had another name.

He was called Jim Thorpe.

In just 12 years, Jim's dream would come true. This great-great grandson of the Sauk warrior Black Hawk would lead the Carlisle football team to one of the greatest victories in sports history.

Jim Thorpe loved to hunt and fish and to ride horses near his home in Indian Territory in what is now Oklahoma. He spent long afternoons running and chasing his dogs along the banks of the Canadian River.

But Jim didn't much care for school. He ran away often. He even ran away from Haskell several times.

Jim's father, Hiram, finally decided to send him to Carlisle Industrial School when Jim was 16. Maybe there, more than a thousand miles from home, Jim would settle down and learn a trade.

Carlisle had been created by the military in 1879 to educate the children of American Indians.

The American government took Native children from their homes and sent them to boarding schools far away. The children were forced to march and to learn trades, like baking or blacksmithing.

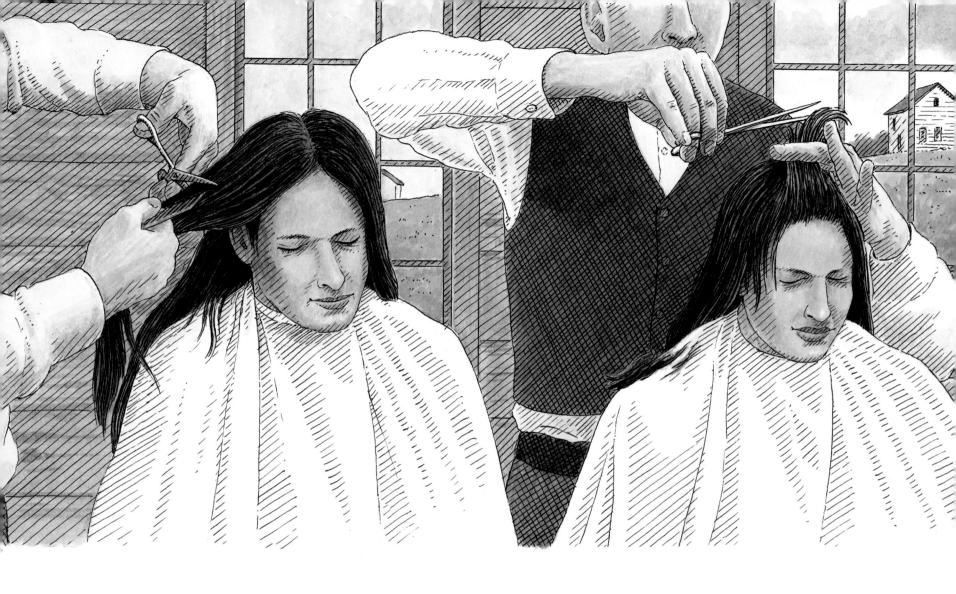

The schools cut the children's hair and burned their traditional clothes. Teachers would not allow them to speak their languages or to practice their religions, often beating the students for doing so.

Like many boys at Carlisle,
Jim worked on a nearby farm
to earn extra money during
the school year.

One day, while walking home from work, Jim saw the boys' track team practicing the high jump. Standing there in his overalls and work boots, the scrawny teenager watched the athletes trying to jump over a bar set between two posts. The bar was set just over Jim's head—five feet, nine inches above the grass. None of the boys could jump over it without knocking it from its posts.

"Can I try?" Jim asked.

The other boys laughed at him.

"Go ahead," one of them said, looking at his big boots and dusty work clothes.

Jim laced up a borrowed pair of track shoes. He trotted up to the bar and jumped, kicking his legs as he had seen the others do.

When he landed in the sand pit on the other side, the bar still rested on its posts. He had cleared it.

Jim picked himself up and brushed off his overalls. He turned to the track team and laughed. Then he returned the shoes and walked away.

Later another boy came to Jim's room. He told him that Glenn "Pop" Warner, coach of the Carlisle track and football teams, wanted to see him.

Jim walked slowly into Coach Warner's office. Looking down at his own feet, Jim asked, "Have I done anything wrong?"

"Son, you've only broken the school record in the high jump," Coach Warner said. "That's all."

Pop Warner handed Jim a uniform and said, "I'll see you at practice tomorrow."

Jim loved all sports. He was fast. He could jump high and far. He could run all day without getting tired, it seemed. And he was tough. He shined in baseball, lacrosse, track, hockey, and football.

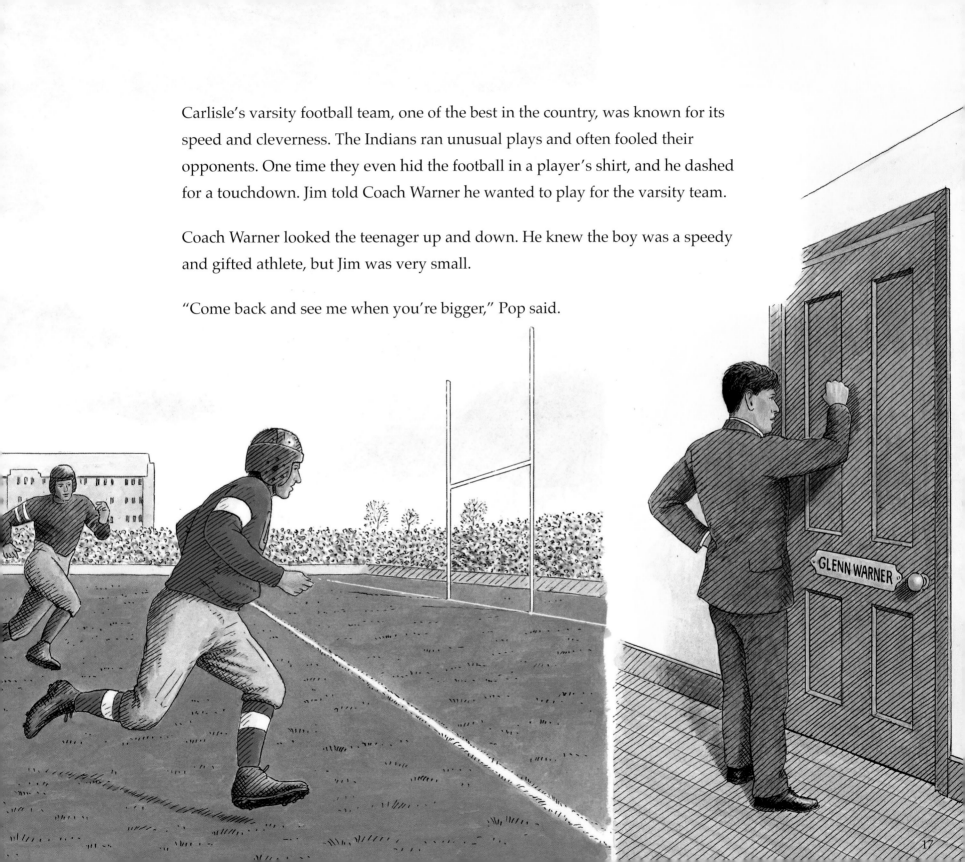

Carlisle's varsity football team, one of the best in the country, was known for its speed and cleverness. The Indians ran unusual plays and often fooled their opponents. One time they even hid the football in a player's shirt, and he dashed for a touchdown. Jim told Coach Warner he wanted to play for the varsity team.

Coach Warner looked the teenager up and down. He knew the boy was a speedy and gifted athlete, but Jim was very small.

"Come back and see me when you're bigger," Pop said.

GLENN WARNER

Jim was not discouraged. For months he trained and he ran. He also grew.

In the fall Jim again begged Coach Warner to put him on the varsity team.

Pop stood on the sidelines as his team practiced. He still thought Jim was too small, but he decided to give him a chance. He tossed him a football and told him to run out on the field to give the team some "tackling practice." The varsity players roared and ran at Jim. He cut and dodged as bigger players tried to tackle him. He ran the length of the field and into the end zone without being tackled.

Jim trotted back to Pop Warner. He smiled as he tossed the football to the coach.

Pop was mad. He thought Jim was pretty full of himself. He told him to do it again as he slammed the football into Jim's middle.

So Jim did.

Pop Warner knew when he was licked. He added Jim to the varsity team.

Jim played football for two seasons before he left school again. After he left Carlisle, he played baseball in North Carolina for a while. When the season was over, he hunted and fished on the Sac and Fox reservation east of Oklahoma City. He also helped to take care of his brothers and sisters. Life was pretty good. He decided he was done with school.

But Pop found him and asked him to come back to Carlisle. He told Jim he would help him train for the 1912 Olympics if he returned. Jim decided to give Carlisle another chance.

By 1912, 25-year-old Jim Thorpe was a star of the Carlisle football team. He had been named to the All-America team in 1911.

Pop Warner kept his promise and traveled with Jim and the U.S. team to Sweden for the summer Olympics.

On his first day of competition, Jim won four of the five events in the pentathlon—the long jump, discus throw, 200-meter sprint, and 1,500-meter race. His gold medal in the pentathlon was the first ever won by an American Indian.

A week later Jim competed in the 10 events of the decathlon over two days. Before the events of the second day, Jim discovered that someone had stolen his shoes. He found a mismatched pair in a trash can and wore them to compete. One shoe was so big, he had to wear several socks to keep it on his foot as he ran.

Even with shoes that didn't fit, Jim won four of the 10 decathlon events. Near the end of the second day, he set a record for the 1,500-meter race—running it in 4 minutes, 40.1 seconds. No decathlete would beat that record for 60 years. Jim won his second gold medal and was declared the greatest athlete in the world.

Jim and Pop sailed back to the United States and their greatest football season.

Because Carlisle was a military base, the school could not charge admission to its games. So Jim's team traveled to colleges all over the country to earn money for the Carlisle program. The home teams paid Carlisle to play because they drew large crowds. Few people in the college towns had ever seen an American Indian.

In 1912 the Indians would play the best teams in the country. Their biggest challenge would come from the United States Military Academy at West Point, where future Army officers trained. The two teams had played only once before, back in 1905. Sportswriters described the 1912 game as a rematch between the Army and Indians who had fought on the battlefield just 20 years before.

Carlisle came into the game undefeated with the best offense in the nation, averaging nearly 40 points a game. The West Point Cadets had the best defense and had lost just one of four games that season. Most people expected the bigger, stronger, better-equipped Army team to handle Carlisle easily. Many sportswriters thought Army had beaten tougher teams and would prove too much for Jim and his teammates.

But Carlisle was playing a new kind of football. The small, quick team did not rely on strength. The players used their speed and their brains to win. They invented plays, like end runs and reverses, that had never been tried before. Carlisle was one of the first teams to throw forward passes.

And Carlisle had Jim Thorpe, the greatest athlete in the world, as its captain.

Thousands of excited fans sat in the stands in the cold, gray late afternoon at West Point. A stiff wind blew out of the northwest as the Carlisle players and their coaches trudged to the visitors' locker room.

As they laced up their shoes and held their stiff leather helmets in their laps, the Indian men turned their eyes to Pop Warner.

The coach walked between the hard wooden benches. He was not much for speeches. But today Pop was excited.

"Your fathers and your grandfathers are the ones who fought their fathers," he said, gesturing toward the field. "These men playing against you today are soldiers. They are the Long Knives. You are Indians. Tonight we will know if you are warriors."

It's true that the Army team was made up of future military leaders. In Army's backfield were four future generals, including Dwight Eisenhower. Forty years later Eisenhower would be elected president of the United States.

The Indians had a few new tricks in store for Army. As they lined up for their first play, they did so in a "double wing" formation. The halfbacks moved up near the line of scrimmage. The defense did not know who might get the snap and what he might do with the ball. Carlisle ran to within yards of the Army end zone several times in the first half. But they couldn't get across the goal line.

Army scored the first touchdown but missed the extra point. The score was 6-0.
But Army's good fortune would not last.

During the third quarter, Jim caught a punt near midfield. Just like the day he ran
through the whole Carlisle squad at "tackling practice," he zigged and zagged his
way up the field. He dashed to the end zone, but a penalty took the touchdown
away. Still, Jim and Carlisle had taken over the game.

Army threw everything they had at Jim. Two linebackers double-teamed the great athlete. Their assignment was to stop him, but he proved unstoppable.

Jim broke free for several 20-yard runs, scattering tacklers with ease. His long runs and amazing pass receptions set up four touchdowns by teammates Alex Arcasa and Joe Bergie. It was Jim's greatest game as a Carlisle player.

WEST POINT 6
CARLISLE 27

When time ran out on the field, the Carlisle Indians shouted and patted each other on the shoulders. They had beaten the Army Cadets, 27-6.

The team was excited as they boarded the train for home. Although tired and bruised, the players couldn't stop laughing and talking about the game. They agreed the victory over Army was the hardest and best game they had ever played.

Quarterback Gus Welch looked at his roommate, Jim Thorpe, and smiled, remembering every hit and tackle. "That," he said, "was the rattling of the bones."

— JIM THORPE —

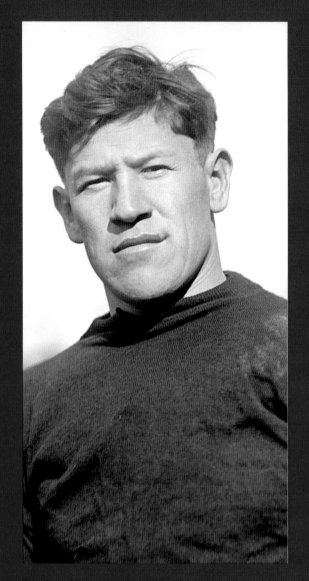

Jim Thorpe was born May 28, 1888, in Indian Territory near what is now Prague, Oklahoma. While he would grow to be one of the greatest athletes of all time, his early life was filled with sadness and tragedy. His father, Hiram, often beat Jim and his brothers and sisters. When Jim was just 9 years old, his twin brother Charlie died of pneumonia. Two years later his mother died after giving birth. Shortly after he arrived at Carlisle at age 16, Jim lost his father too.

Jim often ran away from boarding school, sometimes to return home to care for his brothers and sisters. Other times he left school to work or to play professional sports. Jim was a natural athlete. His track and football careers at Carlisle and his Olympic gold medals earned him the admiration of much of the world. But a stint playing for a professional baseball team in North Carolina in 1910 would later cost him his Olympic medals—because Olympic officials claimed he had given up his amateur status.

Jim excelled at every sport he played. He moved with a natural grace and was very strong. He even won a national ballroom dancing championship with his girlfriend the same year he competed in the Olympics.

After he left school for good, Jim played professional baseball and football. He also coached an NFL team made up entirely of American Indian players, and he was the first president of the American Professional Football Association, now known as the National Football League.

Jim died in 1953, a decade before he was named to the Pro Football Hall of Fame. In 1982 the International Olympic Committee restored Jim's gold medals and gave them to his children.

OTHER MEMBERS OF THE 1912 CARLISLE INDIANS
★ VARSITY FOOTBALL TEAM ★

Alex Arcasa, 21, Colville from Washington, played right halfback and backup quarterback. After his school days, Arcasa stayed in Pennsylvania and worked in a boiler shop.

Joseph Bergie, 20, Turtle Mountain Ojibwe from North Dakota, played center. After Carlisle, Bergie played football at Stanford University.

Elmer Busch, 22, Pomo from California, played right guard. In 1922, Busch played for Coach Jim Thorpe in the inaugural season of the NFL's Oorang Indians.

Pedro "Pete" Calac, 19, Rincon Band of Luiseno Indians from California, played right tackle. He had a 10-year career in the NFL after he was wounded in action during World War I.

William Garlow, 22, Tuscarora from New York, played left guard. After Garlow left Carlisle, he played professional baseball.

Joseph "Big Chief" Guyon, 20, White Earth Ojibwe from Minnesota, played left tackle. The *New York Herald* and the *New York Item* picked him as an All-American tackle in his first year of playing football. After he left Carlisle, Guyon played football in college and for several NFL teams. He was inducted into the Pro Football Hall of Fame in 1966 and the College Football Hall of Fame in 1971.

Robert Hill, 22, Tuscarora from New York, played left guard. After Carlisle, he played for the Oorang Indians.

Roy Large, 19, a Shoshone from Wyoming, played left end. Large served as a sergeant in the U.S. Army during World War I.

Stancil "Possum" Powell, 21, Eastern Band of Cherokee Indians from North Carolina, played fullback. After he was wounded in action in World War I, Powell played professional football for the Oorang Indians.

George "Cotton" Vetternack, 21, Lac du Flambeau Ojibwe from Wisconsin, played right end. He played two years for Coach Jim Thorpe's Oorang Indians before returning home to his reservation.

Gustave "Gus" Welch, 21, Lac Courte Oreilles Ojibwe from Wisconsin, played quarterback. After Carlisle, Welch graduated from Dickinson Law School before enlisting in the Army. He was the first American Indian to make the rank of captain in the U.S. Army. He also had a distinguished career as a college football coach after playing in the NFL.

Joel Wheelock, 22, Oneida from Wisconsin, played in the backfield. After Carlisle, Wheelock graduated from Lebanon Valley College, served in World War I, and worked as a professional athlete, band director, and journalist.

Charles Williams, 21, Caddo from Oklahoma, played end and tackle. After Carlisle, Williams attended Haskell Institute.

POP WARNER

Glenn Scobey "Pop" Warner, who coached college football for more than 40 years, invented many of the plays and formations used by football teams today. Trained as a lawyer at Cornell, Warner was given the nickname Pop in his senior year by the younger players on Cornell's football team.

After college Warner practiced law for only a few months before deciding to make his career in sports. In addition to Carlisle, Warner coached at Cornell, Georgia, Pittsburgh, Stanford, and Temple. He coached twice at Carlisle, from 1899 to 1903 and 1907 to 1914.

He was fired from Carlisle after the 1914 season when players complained about his swearing and abusive treatment. In 1915 he was hired by Pittsburgh, where he would go on to win three national championships. He would add a fourth at Stanford, which he also led to three Rose Bowl appearances. In 1933 the organizers of a youth football league in Pennsylvania renamed the organization the Pop Warner Youth Football League.

CARLISLE INDIAN INDUSTRIAL SCHOOL

The U.S. Army founded the Carlisle Indian Industrial School in Pennsylvania in 1879 as an experiment. The wanted to see if they could make Indian children abandon their ways of life by forcing them to speak English, learn a trade, and go to Christian religious services. Richard Henry Pratt, Carlisle's founder, believed that he must "kill the Indian to save the man."

The boarding schools cut the children's hair, made them dress in strange uniforms, and gave them English names. Children were punished for speaking their own languages and forbidden to practice their traditional religions. Attendance at these boarding schools was mandatory. Some of the children were taken from their families by force. Later some families chose to send their children to boarding schools. Sometimes boarding schools were the only choice Indians had for formal education. Many children died at these boarding schools from malnourishment, disease, and mistreatment. More than 500 students died at Carlisle or soon after they left. More than 200 children are buried at Carlisle, many in unmarked graves.

The boarding school era lasted more than 100 years and included more than 150 schools across the United States. American Indian boarding school enrollment peaked at 60,000 in 1973. By the time Carlisle closed in 1918, more than 10,000 children had attended the school. But in the 39 years it was open, Carlisle graduated just 158 students.

GLOSSARY

All-America—the College Football All-America Team is named annually and made up of the best college football players at each position

backfield—the area behind the offensive and defensive lines in football; also a general name for the players who line up there, such as quarterbacks, halfbacks, and fullbacks

boarding school—a school where students live and learn during the school year

cadets—students who attend the U.S. Military Academy at West Point; also the nickname of their sports teams

decathlon—a modern Olympic sport made up of 10 track and field events; over the years, the 10 events have changed

dress parade—a parade in full dress uniform, often associated with the military

end run—a football play in which the ball carrier tries to run around the end of the line

Indian Territory—land set aside by the U.S. government to resettle American Indians by force; Indian Territory originally included much of the central United States, but over time it shrank to what is now the state of Oklahoma

Long Knives—a name given to American soldiers by some American Indians; the name comes from the swords carried by soldiers

reverse—an offensive play in football in which a back moving in one direction gives the ball to a player moving in the opposite direction

FURTHER READING

Bruchac, Joseph. *Jim Thorpe's Bright Path*. New York: Lee & Low Books, 2008.

Editors of Sports Illustrated Kids. *Football: Then to Wow!* New York: Sports Illustrated Kids, 2014.

Sheinkin, Steve. *Undefeated: Jim Thorpe and the Carlisle Indian School Football Team*. New York: Roaring Brook Press, 2017.

INTERNET SITES

Use FactHound to find Internet sites related to this book.

Visit www.facthound.com

Just type in 9781543504064 and go.

SELECT BIBLIOGRAPHY

"Carlisle Carries Off High-Score Mark for 1912 Football Season." *The Carlisle Arrow* (Carlisle, Penn.). 20 Dec. 1912.

Cress, Joseph. "Carlisle vs. Army: 100 years later, game remembered for celebrity players." *The Sentinel* (Carlisle, Penn.). 8 Nov. 2012.

"Indians Crush West Point." *The Carlisle Arrow*. 15 Nov. 1912.

Jenkins, Sally. *The Real All Americans: The Team That Changed a Game, a People, a Nation*. New York: Doubleday, 2007.

Jenkins, Sally. "The Team That Invented Football." *Sports Illustrated*. 19 April 2007.

"Jim Thorpe Beats the Army." *The New York Times*. 9 Nov. 1912.

Mills, Nicolaus. "How His West Point Football Experience Inspired Eisenhower." Daily Beast. 11 Nov. 2014. 1 Aug. 2017. https://www.thedailybeast.com/how-his-west-point-football-experience-inspired-eisenhower

"World's Greatest Athlete." Pro Football Hall of Fame. 1 Aug. 2107. http://www.profootballhof.com/players/jim-thorpe/

ABOUT —THE— AUTHOR

Art Coulson, Cherokee, was an award-winning journalist and the first executive director of the Wilma Mankiller Foundation in Oklahoma. His first children's book, *The Creator's Game: A Story of Baaga'adowe/ Lacrosse* (Minnesota Historical Society Press, 2013), told of the deep spiritual and cultural connections of American Indian people to the sport of lacrosse. Art still plays traditional Cherokee stickball, an original version of lacrosse, when he is visiting friends and family in the Cherokee Nation of Oklahoma. Art lives in Apple Valley, Minnesota, with his wife and two daughters.

Unstoppable is published by
Capstone Editions, a Capstone imprint,
1710 Roe Crest Drive, North Mankato, Minnesota 56003
www.mycapstone.com

Library of Congress Cataloging-in-Publication Data
Names: Coulson, Art, 1961- author. | Hardcastle, Nick, 1957- illustrator.
Title: Unstoppable : how Jim Thorpe and the Carlisle Indian School defeated the Army / by Art Coulson : illustrated by Nick Hardcastle.
Description: North Mankato, Minnesota : Capstone Editions, 2019. |
Series: Encounter. Narrative nonfiction picture books | Includes bibliographical references and index. | Audience: Age 6-10.
Identifiers: LCCN 2018001952 (print) | LCCN 2018006990 (ebook) |
ISBN 9781543504071 (eBook PDF) | ISBN 9781543504064 (hardcover) |
ISBN 9781543504132 (paperback)
Subjects: LCSH: Thorpe, Jim, 1887-1953—Juvenile literature. | United States
Indian School (Carlisle, Pa.)—Football—History—Juvenile literature. |
United States Military Academy—Football—History—Juvenile literature.
Classification: LCC GV697.T5 (ebook) | LCC GV697.T5 C68 2019 (print) | DDC
796.092 [B] —dc23
LC record available at https://lccn.loc.gov/2018001952

Photo credits:
Library of Congress Prints and Photographs Division/George Grantham Bain Collection, 38,
Harris & Ewing Collection, 36, Panoramic Photographs/Haines Photo Co. (Conneaut, Ohio), 38-39
Design Elements:
Shutterstock: KariDesign

Book design by Russell John Griesmer

Thanks to our adviser for her expertise, research, and advice:
Katrina Phillips, PhD, assistant professor of history at
Macalester College in St. Paul, MN